AF271771

On the Cross

Devotional Poems

The poems in this volume are mostly a result of viewing the crosses made by Paul Friesen for two Methodist churches and two Mennonite churches. The poems are a tribute to his religious art that gives new meanings to the central Christian symbol.

Special thanks to
Ericka Kirstin Wiebe, Ami Regier, Hildi Tiessen,
Jeff Gundy, Jean Janzen, James B. Stucky, and Jeffrey Hillard.

A special greeting and thanks to
Mary Helen Wade of the Science Ridge Mennonite Church,
Sterling, Illinois.

Ohio Arts Council

Supported by a grant from the Ohio Arts Council

The DreamSeeker
Poetry Series

Books in the DreamSeeker Poetry Series, intended to make available fine writing by Anabaptist-related poets, are published by Cascadia Publishing House under the DreamSeeker Books imprint and often copublished with Herald Press. Cascadia oversees content of these poetry collections in collaboration with DreamSeeker Poetry Series Editor Jean Janzen as well as in consultation with its Editorial Council and the authors themselves.

1. On the Cross
   By Dallas Wiebe, 2005
2. I Saw God Dancing
   By Cheryl Denise Miller, 2005
3. Evening Chore
   By Shari Miller Wagner, 2005

Also worth noting are two poetry collections that would likely have been included in the series had it been in existence then:

1. Empty Room with Light
   By Ann Hostetler, 2002
2. A Liturgy for Stones
   By David Wright, 2003

On the Cross

Devotional Poems

Dallas Wiebe

Line drawings by
John Leon

Line drawings based on crosses by
Paul Friesen

DreamSeeker Poetry Series, Volume 1

DreamSeeker Books
TELFORD, PENNSYLVANIA

an imprint of
Cascadia Publishing House

Copublished with
Herald Press
Scottdale, Pennsylvania

Cascadia Publishing House orders, information, reprint permissions:
contact@CascadiaPublishingHouse.com
1-215-723-9125
126 Klingerman Road, Telford PA 18969
www.CascadiaPublishingHouse.com

On the Cross
Copyright © 2005 by Cascadia Publishing House
Telford, PA 18969
All rights reserved
DreamSeeker Books is an imprint of Cascadia Publishing House
Copublished with Herald Press, Scottdale, PA
Library of Congress Catalog Number: 2004027795
ISBN: 1-931038-27-9
Book design by Cascadia Publishing House
Cover design by Gwen M. Stamm
All line drawings, including cover, copyright © John Leon and
based on cross designs © Paul Friesen

The paper used in this publication is recycled and meets the
minimum requirements of American National Standard for Information
Sciences—Permanence of Paper for Printed Library Materials, ANSI Z39.48-1984.1984

Some of these poems have been published in the following places:
"A Note to Paul Friesen," "Pietà" and "On Bearing the Sign of Christ into the
New Millenium," *Mennonite Life* (December, 2002, online only); "My Pectoral
Cross," "At the Foot of the Cross," "At Easter," "Yea, Though I Walk" and
"Raise High the Crossbeams, Carpenters," *The Conrad Grebel Review* (Winter,
2003), 105-110. "Georg Trakl's Psalm" first appeared in a slightly different ver-
sion in *The Sixties* (Spring, 1966), 36-39.

Library of Congress Cataloguing-in-Publication Data
Wiebe, Dallas E.
  On the cross : devotional poems / Dallas Wiebe ; line drawings by John Leon ;
line drawings based on crosses by Paul Friesen.
    p. cm. -- (DreamSeeker poetry series ; v. 1)
  ISBN 1-931038-27-9 (pbk. : alk. paper)
  1. Jesus Christ--Crucifixion--Poetry. 2. Christian poetry, American. I. Title.
II. Series.
  PS3573.I3O5 2005
  811'.54--dc22

                                                    2004027795

12 11 10 09 08   10 9 8 7 6 5 4 3 2

For Viriginia (Schroeder) Wiebe
October 15, 1929-April 19, 2002

Contents

List of Illustrations

All crosses designed by Paul Friesen, Hesston, Kansas; and rendered in line drawings by John Leon. Used by permission, all rights reserved.

Going to the Cross

It's not easy to find.
It's somewhere in the vast waste land
  between you and God.
Many have failed in the journey.
Many have died along the way.
Many have sat down and wept
  because they can't see the tiny light
  that radiates from the axletree
  over beyond the borders of darkness.
The tiny light says, "Stand up and walk.
  Don't sit and weep. It's worth
  the trouble to get there."
The light says, "I'm just one step away
  if you go in the right direction."
The light says, "Come unto me
  and I will give you rest."
The cross is somewhere across the vast waste land
  between you and God.
Follow the path, one step at a time,
  and you will find it.
Follow the tiny light
  that beckons in your soul.

*The chancel sculpture is
made up of three crosses which
symbolize the crosses of
(1) atonement,
(2) redemption, and
(3) rejection.*

*The intent of the work
is not to provide decoration but to
inspire provocative medition on
confronting the One who is Life,
Light, and Love.*

--Paul Friesen

The Cross of Atonement

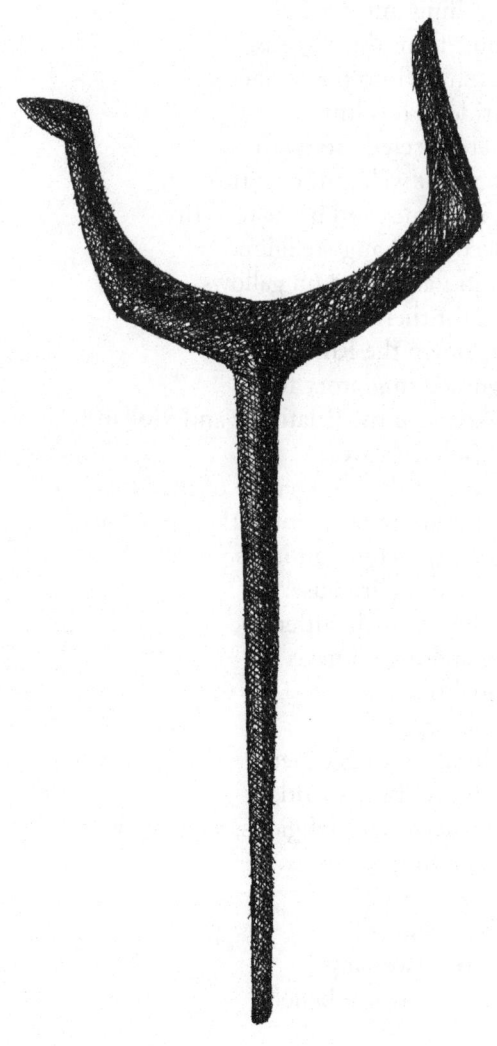

The Anabaptist Radiance

We are marching, marching upward
 into the afterglow of our ancestors.
We are marching into the light
 that streams from their words.
We are marching into the radiance
 of Bible-ridden revolution.
They gathered secretly to reaffirm
 that all was not well in the world.
They met in homes and barns to verify
 that they could change religion.
They died in flames and on gallows
 to witness for their souls.
They came down the Rhine River
 like misguided migratory fowl.
They sneaked into the Palatinate and Holland
 like unwanted relatives.
They hid among the bourgeoisie of the North Sea
 until even Rembrandt painted their portraits.
Now they are marching on in us,
 the progeny of their abuse,
 the pale glow of their suffering.
They are marching on in us
 in our squabbling,
 in our schisms,
 in our refusals of each other,
 in our refusals of the world,
 and in our persistent, religious democracy.
They are marching on in us
 to tell the world
 that we have choices,
 that we can all worship
 according to our own beliefs.

They are marching to say
that if there is no free will
then nothing matters.
The radiance of the Anabaptists
still shines out in our lives
when we say to those about us,
"Not us, friends. Not us."

Christmas Eve, 1998

It's a first for us;
Christmas Eve alone.
My wife and I sit
  and wonder
What to do
To greet a savior's birth
  by ourselves
  in silence and old age.
No singing, no children, no tree.
Even the Christmas star
  is obscured
  by the city's lights and haze.
None of the Christmas players were alone;
  the shepherds, the wise men,
  the holy family.
The joy of birth was shared.
Old and dying, we sit alone,
  knowing no one is going to come
  to bless our child.
No one is on his way
  with gifts of gold,
  frankincense and myrrh.
We know there are no angels
  on the wing,
No merry host over our stable.
In our silent night,
  there's nothing holy
  about loneliness,
Unless it's the Cross.

The Cross of Redemption

Take Up Your Cross and Follow Me

How is that possible?
Who could bear the weight,
And who knows how to follow?
The cross alone would break your back,
And the long haul in the following
   would be beyond measure.
The cross alone would drive you down
   into the dirt of the road,
And the following would be dusty and hot.
The cross alone would be as heavy as nails,
   and the way after would be as long as a spear.
To pick it up is not an act of courage.
To pick it up is not an act of will.
To pick it up is an act of grace.
The wood is splintered.
The nails are iron.
The sign at the top
   has your name on it.
You must lift it without fear.
You must crawl with it
   until you drop.
You must lie under it
   until lifted up.
Where is my cross?
Where is the road to follow?
Where are the splinters and the dust?
I'm ready.
Show me where it is
   and I'll take it up,
   no matter how heavy
   and how far.

Lift High the Cross

That's easy for you to say,
  you who never played *Scrabble* in the dark,
  you who never swam the Mississippi River,
  you who never knelt at a computer.
Besides, anyone can take up a cross
  if he has corporate sponsors.
Anyone can take up a cross
  if he has attack helicopters on alert.
Anyone can take up a cross
  if he has nuclear weapons in his pocket.
The cross is heavy for the poor.
The cross is crushing for the defenseless.
The cross is devastating for the dying.
Impossible, you say?
I'd as soon defend Afghanistan
  as take up a cross.
I'd as soon be a Palestinian
  in the Gaza Strip
  as lift it to my shoulders.
I'd as soon be a congressman
  as to pick its splinters
  from my rotting brain.
Take it up, you say.
Lift it high and walk.
Set your feet towards Calvary
  before you collapse into the street,
  before you collapse into the dust,
  before you collapse into darkness.

Crucifixion with a View of Toledo by El Greco (1541-1614)

The cross was made by a carpenter.
It's solid, good wood, functional,
  a machine for execution.
Toledo and bones lie around the foot of the cross.
Over the dying man's head
  a sign in Hebrew, Greek and Latin
  tells us who is crucified,
Who it is who looks upward,
Whose expression says, "You're kidding,"
Whose beard and mustache are trimmed,
Whose crown of thorns is stylish,
Whose loincloth is well laundered.
The body is well lighted.
The sky is dark with flashes of light.
Christ seems well fed and comfortable.
It's a painting by someone
  who never felt pity or shame.
It's a painting by a sexless monk,
  an exercise in ordered devotion.
El Greco's cross will not splinter into relics.
It will not topple in an earthquake.
It will not rot
  so it is reusable as beams in a house.

Visitors to the museum
  where the painting hangs
Will not be disturbed
  by the death of a savior.
They will not remark
  upon his failed mission.
No one will weep for the moment
  depicted over a Spanish town.
The visitors will note
  how much the painting is worth
  and let it go at that.

Dali's "*Corpus Hypercubus*": *An Ekphrasis*

The cross is not planted in the earth.
It floats as cubes
  that buoy it up towards heaven.
Gala, as the mother of God,
  kneels in the corner
  and gazes up at her son.
She is not weeping,
  and the body is not bleeding
  as it ascends toward heaven.
His side is not pierced,
  and he is not nailed to the cross
  that reflects the mundane cubes below.
A darkness covers the earth.
A faint light glimmers on the horizon.
Only Christ's shadow is stuck to the cross.
The face of the crucified savior
  is averted
  and there is no crown of thorns.
There is no sign of INRI
  over his brown hair.
There is no hair on his face
  or on his body.
The cubes are the earth
  and he is floating free.
At the foot of the cross,
  Gala does not weep
  because she knows
  he is the light,
  and darkness will be destroyed.
Spreading his light,
  the body of Christ ascends.

Kneeling by the cross,
  the mother does not weep
  because her lovely son
  is not shamed by exposed genitals.
She does not weep
  because she knows
  his hair and her hair
  are the same color.
She does not weep because she
  is heavily clothed
  and he is naked
  in a death
  that transfigures the world.

Matthias Grünewald's "Crucifixion"

The Germans get it right:
"O Haupt voll Blut und Wunden,"
"Mitten wir im Leben sind mit dem Tod umfangen,"
"Christ lag in Todesbanden,"
"Gottes Zeit is die allerbeste Zeit,"
"Auf meines Kindes Tod,"
"Im Abendrot,"
"Liebestod,"
"Ein deutsches Requiem,"
"Selig sind, die da Leid tragen,"
"Denn alles Fleisch es ist wie Gras,"
"Tod und Verklärung,"
"Kindertotenlieder,"
"Der Tod ist ein Meister aus Deutschland,"
And Matthias Grünewald.
The body on his cross is dying
  and there is no doubt about that.
The body is emaciated from scourging,
  loss of blood, pain and thirst.
Nothing pretty on this cross,
  nothing likely to rise from the dead.
And the whole world is dying with him.
That's why the dying man is a savior.
That's why the dying man will redeem the world.
That's why the dying man is the Son of God.

Calvary

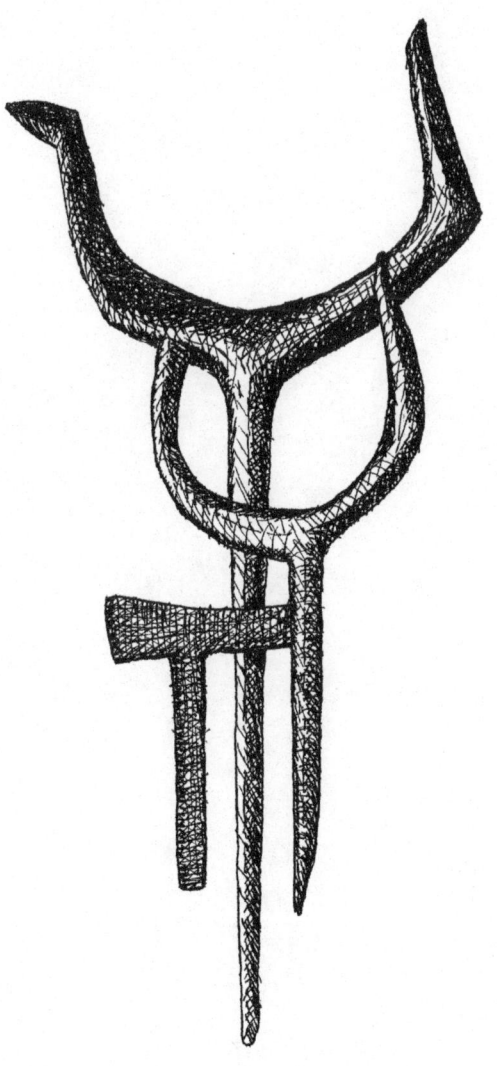

Pietà

At the foot of my cross is me.
At the foot of my cross
  is my navel and my stomach
  and two punctures
  where the tubes entered
  to drain my wounds,
  where for five days water and blood
  came flowing round and out.
At the foot of my cross
  there is no beloved disciple or a weeping mother
  or someone throwing dice for my seamless coat.
My stigmata are hidden
  so no one can see where I was pierced.
They will be manifest only
  when I get my loincloth and my crown of thorns.
Even so, no one will cradle my body and carry it
  to a rock enclosure.
Nor will I rise on a third day.
I will not noodle along to Emmaus.
I will not appear in Galilee.
No one will take my death
  to be the good news of salvation.
At the foot of my cross is me,
  and behind it
  and above it
  and all around
  that fragile stick.

At Easter

What is that breeze
  that comes from Calvary?
What is that soft wind
  that comes from the north,
  the east, the south and the west?
What is that derelict air
  that filters down to us?
It is the air that carries
  the clamor of the Romans and the priests.
It is the gentle wind that carries
  the gossip at the foot of the cross.
It is the breeze that carries
  the timid whispering from the top.
It's springtime in Jerusalem.
The summer is coming in.
It is time for harvesting and good food.
It's the time of hot days and chilled nights.
It's the time of palm branches
  and the shedding of cloaks.
It's the time of crowing cocks.
The breeze soothes the holy mount.
It washes the citizens in comfort.
It makes them smile at men on donkeys.
What is that breeze that never ceases?
It is the breath
  that comes from Golgotha.
It arrives upon your fears.
It tells you more
  than you want to know.
It rings in your ears.

The Crucifix

The surgeon opened my chest
  and entered my heart.
He fixed my rude mechanicals
  and left upon my chest
  a scar in the shape of a cross.
The great dividing moment in time
  now rides on my skin,
A cross over my heart
  never to be removed,
Never to be brought down
  until I die,
Never to be loaded
  with a dying savior.
My cross I'll bear
  into my new world.
My cross I'll suffer
  into my eternity.
My cross that will not
  let me forget
That moment God tried
  to save us all.

My Pectoral Cross

It's not much of a cross
  but it will have to do.
The surgeon who cracked my chest
  didn't have a lot of choice
  as to how to close the wound.
The sternum and the ribs
  determined his design
When he sewed me shut
  and said, "Voilà."
My primary care physician
  once told me I have a "soft heart."
And I do for doctors
  who cut us up.
I have a soft heart
  for the knives that slit and slice,
  for the hands that fondle and peel
  our internal organs,
  for the machines
  that let us live again
  after a short death.
The Giacometti cross fills my chest
  and draws the skin into it.
The cross swells and contracts
  with my breath.

The cross rides out in advance
  of all my going and coming.
I bear my cross alone and gladly.
Thin and lined with dead blood,
  it blesses me under my shirt.
No one would know my pectoral cross was there
  if my stumbling and falling
  didn't mark my path
  towards the first Crucifixion.

Handiwork

The hand of the surgeon
  became like the hand of God
When the surgeon cut
  the sign of salvation
  into my chest.
When the surgeon opened my chest
  he looked into my heart
  the way God must look
  when he scrutinizes humankind.
When the surgeon found something amiss
  he, like God, repaired the faulty heart
  and gave it another chance at life.
Even so, the chirurgeon, the handworker,
  by his chiromancy,
  undid the first flaw,
  the corrupt nature of the human heart.
Even so came Christ, the everlasting light.
Even so, by man came death;
  by God and chirurgery came life.
One made the faulty heart;
The other cleaned up the mess.
In chirurgery the handiwork of healing,
A second chance at life,
Like sending a son to die
  for a horrible mistake.

On Bearing the Sign of Christ Into the New Millennium

The surgeon's knife cut just in time
  to get that cross on my chest
  for the third millennium A.D.
Like a message from the gods,
  he marked me for a mission
  to carry the sign, although hidden,
  into a new age lest the sign
  be lost or forgotten.
My wiry little scar pokes down
  toward my navel.
The crossbeam is short
  and hardly strong enough to hold a body.
No body hangs from the cross
  except mine.
On the back of it
  and out of proportion.
I'm no longer myself,
But the image of an idea.
I'm being used against my will
  to bear the sign.
There's no erasing it.
There's no denying its presence.
There's no escaping what it means.

Punch Lines

There are jokes about the cross.
One ends, "John, I can see your house."
One should end, "Is nothing sacred?"
One punch line to the jokes
  is yet to be realized.
When that final punch line comes,
All humankind will weep for itself,
  will stand at the foot of the cross
  and lower the body into its arms,
  carry it away
  and bury it in stone.
The people will weep,
  the rocks will weep,
  the trees will weep,
  the birds and the sky will weep
And the government upon his shoulders
  will stand dry-eyed
  amongst the rubble
  of Vietnam, Nicaragua, Panama,
  Kosovo, Iraq, Afghanistan, Granada,
  El Salvador, Guatemala, Chile,
  Dominican Republic, Cuba, Kuwait,
  Israel, Cambodia, Laos and Huntsville, Texas.

So anyway, there's this guy who has a son.
He sends him out for bubble gum.
He comes back with a box of globs
  well chewed and full of air.
The salivating chewers talk of
  "Salvation," "Savior" and "Son of Gum."
"Wow," say the dead,
"Where can we get pieces of this gum?"
"Nowhere," I say.
"They fall through the holes in his hands."

Gladly the Cross I'd Bear

Children made a joke of the song
  when they sang it,
Just as they did when they sang
  "While shepherds washed
  their socks by night."
Just as they sang, "Shall we gather at the flivver
  that runs from the Ford garage"
And "Round John virgin."
They sang the lines loud, and loved
  the bear with eye problems,
  the shepherds busy with their laundry,
  the old car sputtering from the repair shop,
  the fat boy who didn't know about sex.
It made a hot Sunday morning
  into an entertainment
Until their happy voices singing out for Jesus
  would finally dwindle to a whisper,
Until their little golden throats would wither
  into skin that hung from their voice boxes
  like pages from dried-out hymnals,

Until they would begin to hum to themselves,
  "Gladly the cross I'd bear,"
And get every word right,
Until they'd hum it with all its meaning
  and know that "gladly"
  had nothing to do with it,
Until they'd lift their cracking voices
  and realize that the cross never ends,
Realize that whether in joy or sorrow
  it looms over our lives
  as we watch our flocks by night,
  gather at the river that flows
  from the throne of God,
  and gaze at Mary in her agony,
Until they'd realize that the cross
  hangs over our days
  until we all flow down from it
  in water and blood.

On a Hill Faraway

The old rugged cross
  she ain't what she used to be.
You see those crosses made nowadays
  by people who went to art school
And you wonder,
  "What happened to the body?
  What happened to the mother?
  What happened to the wood?
  Where are the Romans, the dice,
  the nails, the punctured side,
  the INRI, the water and the blood?"
Those artsy-craftsy people have made Christ
  into a fashion statement,
Who hangs there like an unbaptised model
  who never rode a donkey,
  tried on a crown of thorns,
  or pushed away a stone.
He shines there like an ad
  in *The New Yorker.*
Let's try it again:
The old rugged cross
  she hitched to our redemption
  many long years ago.

For a World of Lost Sinners

The old rugged cross stood on Golgotha,
  on that hill far away,
And carried the load of centuries of guilt,
  stood up under the wind and sand,
  leaned not a bit in weakness
    when the sins of the world dropped upon it
    like rocks from the heavens.
The old rugged cross raised high its beam
  and carried the suffering Christ
  into future years of redemption and grace.
Now the old rugged cross
  is only a song at Easter, sometimes.
It's only a memory
  on a Sunday School picture card.
Its yoke is easy
  and its burden is light
  for those who cannot see
  the body on that axletree
Nor the flood of grace
  that runs from the nails
  driven through the flesh.

The Light of the World

Break forth, oh beauteous heavenly light,
  for the world is covered with darkness.
Break forth and tell us a mystery
  before our final extraction.
Break forth before it is too late
  for light, mystery or our fading eyes.

He came as light to the world.
He came as light to everyone of us.
He came as light, free of charge.
We had but to believe
  and the light would break forth
  and remain forever and ever.
Instead of the simple acceptance,
  we built bombs, hate and aggression.
We took the light into the skies
  in laser weapons.
We created a light of our own
  to dash the nations.
We broke forth our own light
  and it was lethal.

The hill of Zion is become a place of wrath.
The hill of Zion is become a place of death.
The hill of Zion is become a place of darkness.
Where once the cross towered over our world,
There is only emptiness and the graves of us all.
Salvation floated in the crown of Christ.
Salvation spewed from the dying savior.
Salvation rippled over our open mouths,
Until the Mount of Zion
  is become as empty as our hardened hearts.

Rock of Ages

In the rifted rock I'm resting,
  waiting for the shadow of the cross
  to pass over me.
In the rifted rock I'm waiting
  for the waters of life to flow around me.
In the rifted rock I'm praying
  for eternal rest and peace.

The shadow of the cross drifts
  across the face of the cliff.
The springs of life pour emptiness
  across the solid stones.
The prayers for salvation bounce off the walls
  and into the passing winds.

No one will know I'm here
  and why I tremble with the shaking stones.
No one will bring me something to drink
  while I gaze out over the edge.
No one will mark my passing
  when the earthquakes end my vigil.

The redeemer ended in stone.
The redeemer waited to rise.
The redeemer walked from his prison.
Why shouldn't I?
His rifted rock was only a passageway
  to eternal glory.
And what for me?
His rifted rock came only after agony.
Why should I complain?
His rifted rock ended up empty.
Why shouldn't mine?

After the short sleep of death,
  he walked to Emmaus.
After the experience of the cold stone
  he appeared in Galilee.
After the finger in the side
  he rose to heaven.
Why shouldn't we?

In the rifted rock I'm resting
  while the rock slides slowly
  towards the pit.

"I'm going to shoulder up my cross,
Going to take it home to Jesus.
Ain't that good news?"

Shouldering up your cross
  isn't good news
Unless your shoulders
  are broader and stronger than mine.
When I pick up my cross
  and lay it on my shoulders
I fall to my knees
  because I can't bear the weight.
And carry it home?
What good is it at home
  where all my sins and griefs abound?
I want to shoulder it up
  and carry it to Golgotha,
  lift it up, climb on
  and hang there forever.
I want to feel the winds of the desert
  blowing through my crown of thorns.
I want to drink the bitter gall
  out of a sponge.
I want to turn on my nails
  that hold me closer to God.
When darkness covers the earth,
  I want to find my way
  into the stone tomb.

When morning breaks
  I want to throw off my rags
  and walk to Emmaus.
When I ascend into heaven
I want to sing a crazy song
  of good news to all the world.
I want to cry out to everyone
  to shoulder up their crosses.
I want to see them stumble and follow me
  as they carry them home to Jesus.

The Old Rugged Cross

It had to be rugged
  to bear the savior
  who carried the sins of the world.
The weight must have been heavier
  than wood can stand
  or man can measure.
The weight must have been heavier
  than all the forests of the world
  and their beams could support.
The weight must have been heavier
  than all the blood and all the water
  for the redeemed world.
No wonder he cried out in thirst
  when the sun doubled his burden.
No wonder he cried out "It is finished"
  when the darkness multiplied his suffering.
No wonder he cried out for God to anoint him
  when the thunder rolled and the lightning flashed
  and the burden drove him from the wood
  and into stone.

In the Cross of Christ I Glory

But that's about it.
Who cares what I think
   about that lost moment
When all the world
   could have been saved?
Who joins me in the glory
   when I'm sitting alone
   in a Canadair Regional jet?
Who rides with me
   as we whistle through the air
   at 30,000 feet?
We all know the answers
   to these questions.
We know, as certain as sin,
   that my glory is just glory.
We know the cross is as present
   as the small rain
   that wavers across the wings.
But if I don't glory in the cross,
   who will?
When we land in Wichita
   I'll hum my way
   through the terminal,
   let the glory fill my limping heart
   and keep the glory to myself
Where it does some good.

Songs

I been buked and I been sorrowed.
I had to walk this lonesome valley.
I had to walk it by myself.
No one else could walk it for me.
I was wounded for your transgressions.
I was laughed to scorn.
When my journey ended
After the buking and the sorrowing,
After the walking in the lonesome valley,
After the wounding and after the laughter,
I arose on the cross
So that the glory of the Lord
  would be revealed to you,
So that you could all see together
  in the flesh
That I was a pilgrim of sorrow.

While you wait in meditation, let these events, and any others the symbol may suggest, be celebrated anew in your life. What you celebrate may not be the same as what your neighbor celebrates. That is to be expected, for God deals with each of us as individuals. And don't be surprised if each time you come, the symbol has something different to say, for you also will have changed.
—Paul Friesen

Science Ridge Cross

Folk Song

Blow the wind southerly, southerly,
Soft over my cross
So that it will gently waver
Like the breath of God
  when He created the earth and the seas.

Blow the wind southerly
So that my cross will bloom
With the scented blossoms
  of roses and daisies
Like the hand of God
  when he calmed the waves.

Blow the wind southerly
So that the thorns will soften,
  the spear will bend,
  the water and the blood will flow gently
Down my side
Like the feet of God
  when he walked upon the mountains,
  when He stepped across the plains,
  when He stood
  by my corroded heart
    and wept.

To the Crucified Christ
After Paul Gerhardt

O wounded and bloody head,
Full of pain and scorn,
O head bound into derision
By a crown of thorns,
O head once beautifully adorned
With highest honors and respect
And now viciously condemned,
I speak a welcome to you.

You, noble face,
That once rejected and drove away
The great weight of the world,
How shamed you are.
How pale you are.
Who has so brutally
Extinguished the light of your eyes
That once no light could equal?

What you suffer now, Lord,
Is all a burden from me.
I myself am guilty
Of what you have to bear.
Look, here I stand, a poor sinner
Who deserves only anger.
Give me, O my savior,
The vision of your grace.

Recognize me, my protector.
My shepherd, lift me up.
From you, source of all goodness,
All good comes to me.
Your voice has filled me
With milk and sweet nourishment.
Your spirit has sated me
With the food of heaven.

I want to stand by you.
Don't reject me.
I will not depart from you
When your heart breaks.
I will cradle you
In my arms and bosom
When your head pales
In the final throes of death.

It is for my happiness
And for my joyful well being
If I find my salvation
In your suffering.
O if I could only give my life, dear life,
To you on the cross.
What a great gift
That would be for me.

I thank you from my heart,
O Jesus, my friend,
For your pains in death
That you so faithfully suffer
And give so that I may remain
Faithful to you,
So that when I die
In you may be my ending.

If ever I should go from you,
Don't abandon me.
When I must suffer death,
Step forward and comfort me.
When my greatest suffering
Shall surround my heart
Take my dread from me
By the power of your dread and pain.

Come forth as my shield,
As comfort in my death,
And let me see again
Your face in your suffering on the cross.
Then I will look to you.
Then I will, full of faith,
Clutch you to my heart.
Who dies that way, dies well.

Nursery Rhyme III

If all the blood was one blood,
   what a great blood that would be.
If all the water was one water,
   what a great water that would be.
If all the spears were one spear,
   what a great spear that would be.
If all the crosses were one cross,
   what a great cross that would be.
If all the saviors were one savior,
   what a great savior that would be.
If all the Romans were one Roman,
   what a great Roman that would be.
And if the great Roman crucified the great savior
   on the great cross
And pierced the side of the great savior
   with the great spear
So that the great water and the great blood
   came flowing down,
Oh what a great redemption that would be.

E. D. on the Cross

Because I Could not—stop the Blood—
I stirred the Dirt—around—
And Washed his Trembling—punctured Feet—
With Soil—from the Ground—

He looked Below—to See the Soul—
That Cared—to ease his Pain—
And saw my fumbling—bloody—Hands—
That flaked away—the Stain—

I raised my Face—to meet his Gaze—
And saw no Tears—of Loss—
His deathly Stare—Assured my Eyes—
His Pain—would never Cease—

Until I Wrapped—my Own soft Lips—
Around—the crooked Nail—
To let Him Know—that he had Died—
To save Us all from Hell—

W. C. W. on the Cross

so much depends
upon

a simple, wooden
cross

glazed with sacred
blood

inside the gathering
darkness.

Crisscross

It's the simplest kind of construction;
Two pieces joined to make a third.
A conflation of simplicities.
Nothing complicated in the design.
Until it's used.
How quickly it all changes.
It only takes a body, some vinegar,
A spear, some darkness,
A few hangers-on,
A rock tomb, some rags and a sunrise
Until those two crossed sticks
Become a religion
And the believers begin killing each other
Over what those two sticks mean.

A Note to Paul Friesen

Making crosses is a slippery business,
  as you surely know.
You'd just as well make them out of water
  as out of wood.
The making of crosses may be more difficult
  than bearing them.
Nobody ever said it would be easy.
The dream of meaning is as fluid
  as the seed from which the tree grows.
The chimera of belief is as foggy
  as the clouds from which the rain comes
  to water the tree.
The hallucination of significance is as empty
  as the air in which the tree flourishes.
Anyone can cross two sticks and say,
  "Look. That's belief."
Anyone can draw a picture and say,
  "Behold. Here's the way it was."
Anyone can write a song and say,
  "That's what it all amounts to."
A cross might say,
  "Come unto me and I will give you rest."
Any cross could say,
  "Behold the lamb of God."
All crosses must say,
  "Here is death. For what it's worth."

When you first touch the wood
   that you will turn into a cross,
   notice the grain that leads to the foot
Where you and I and all mankind stand,
Where the water and the blood drip over us,
Where redemption flourishes
   if we work long enough
   at the wood in our souls
   from which our special crosses are made.

Prince of Peace Chapel Cross

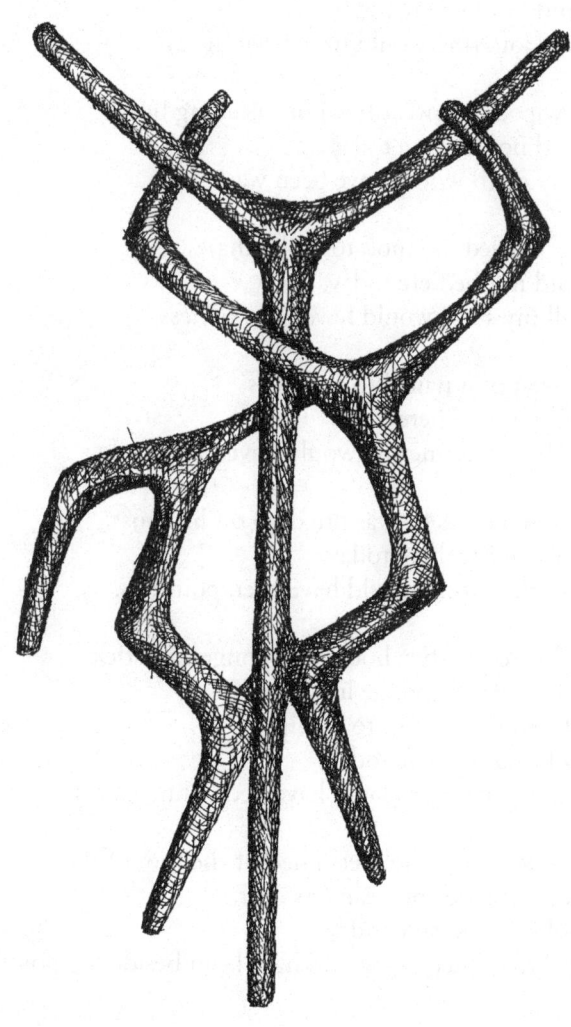

In the Subjunctive

Had I stood on the street in Jerusalem
  and watched him stumble by under his cross,
  I would not be here today
  and my loitering would have been in vain.

Had I wiped the sweat from his bleeding brow,
  I would not be here today
  and my cloth would have been wasted.

Had I followed the mob to Golgotha,
  I would not be here today
  and all my steps would have been useless.

Had I seen him nailed to the cross,
  I would not be here today
  and all the hammering would have been futile.

Had I watched as he was lifted up on his cross,
  I would not be here today
  and all the lifting would have been pointless.

Had I looked as they hooked a sponge to a stick
  and dipped the sponge in vinegar
  and lifted the sponge to his lips,
  I would not be here today
  and all the vinegar would have been unnecessary.

Had I watched the soldiers kneel at the foot of the cross
  and cast dice for his seamless coat,
  I would not be here today
  and all that kneeling would have been beside the point.

Had I listened to his whispered suffering,
 I would not be here today
 and all my listening would have ended in silence.

Had I wiped the water and blood from his side,
 I would not be here today
 and all my cleaning would not have stopped the flow.

Had I lowered him gently from the cross into my arms,
 I would not be here today
 and all my tenderness would have ended once and for all.

Had I put him into the tomb and rolled up the stone,
 I would not be here today
 and all my pushing would have revealed nothing.

Had I gathered the rags from the empty tomb,
 I would not be here today
 and all my gathering would have been forgotten.

Had I walked to Emmaus and waited in Galilee,
 I would not be here today
 and all my walking and waiting would have been for naught.

Had I seen him rise into heaven,
 I would not be here today
 and all my watching would have been wasted.

Had I been there for all that,
 I would not be here today
 and the last witness would not be here
 to tell what it all means.

Raise High the Crossbeams, Carpenters

The view from the top of a cross is endless.
The view from the foot of a cross is uplifting.
The view from now is blank.
No wonder the sun is spent.
No wonder our days drift away.
No wonder the night comes on triumphant.
Who will resurrect the cross
   if not you and you and you?
Who will scan the scenery of salvation
   if not you and you and you?
Who will scatter the blood and water
   from the wound
   if not you and you and you?
Touch the wood.
Feel its warmth.
Caress its splinters.
You will fall for its message.
You will hear its vibrations.
You will blink at its radiations.
Nail the crossbeam to the shaft.
Nail your Savior to the cross.
Nail yourself to his feet.

Raise high the crossbeam
  when the earth quakes
  and the thunder crackles,
  when the birds flee and the winds cavort,
  when the sky opens
  and the lightning comes down.
Maybe then you will see the light.
Maybe then you will know the way.
Maybe then you will kneel and see
  that the nails are loose,
  that the body is irrelevant,
  that the everlasting light
  is in your eyes.

At the Foot of the Cross

They sat on the rocky ground
　and sang above the pain in their legs and rumps.
They sang about Spring and flowers,
　fields of grain and showers of rain.
They talked of his triumphal entry,
　of angry priests and Roman spears.
They worried for the children at home
　and food for the Sabbath.
What else could they do
　in the long day
　from the crown of thorns to Golgotha?
When he said, "Father, forgive them,"
　they looked for forgiveness
　and wondered what he meant.
When he told a thief
　that he'd be in Paradise that day,
　how could they know what he said?
When he whispered, "Behold a son and behold a mother,"
　what were they to gather
　as they looked at each other?
When he cried out in Greek,
　what were they to consider
　without a translation?
When he mentioned thirst,
　what could they offer
　when they had no water?
When he said, "It is finished,"
　what could they do
　but get up
　and go home to supper?

When he commended his spirit to God,
  what could they do
  but leave him to another?
After the long moments of listening
  they wandered to their houses
  and tried to remember what he had said.
After the long hours of pain,
  they washed themselves
  and left him to a different Joseph.
After the long day of singing, gossiping and sweating,
  they hid inside their daily selves
  and waited for the earth to disappear.

Whitestone Mennonite Church Cross

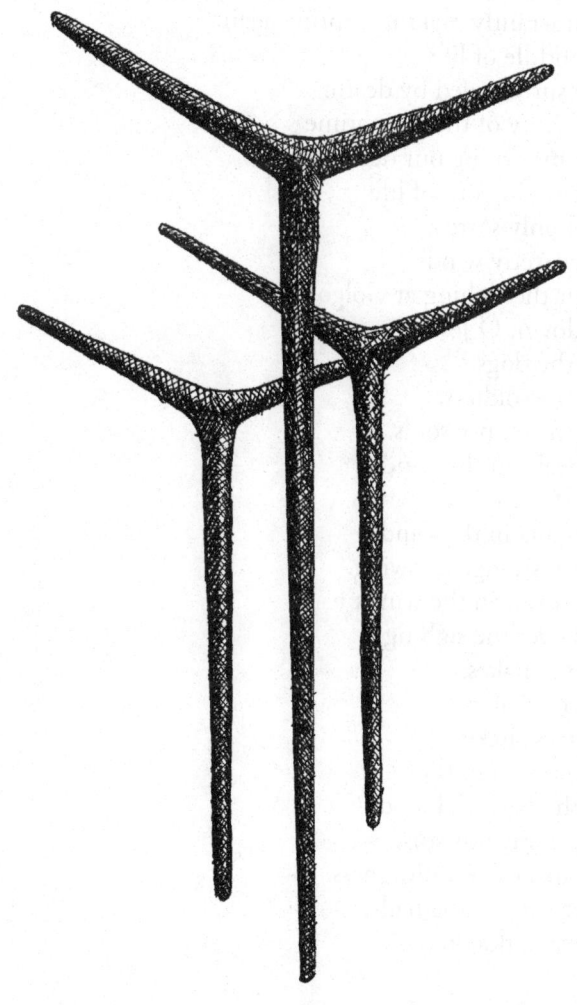

Good Friday's Cross, April 18, 2003

April is in full bloom.
The flowering trees are full of blossoms.
The jonquils, daffodils, hyacinths, tulips,
  are exuberantly making a spring again.
In the middle of life
  we are surrounded by death.
In the beauty of the springtime
  we are mourning our dead.
In the bursting out of life
  we feel only sorrow.
In the westerly winds
  we hear the sighing at Golgotha.
Come down, O Jesus.
Call in the dogs.
Call in the soldiers.
Call in the empty souls.
Who speaks in the winds
  tells a strange tale.
Who shouts in the winds
  reveals a strange knowing.
Who screams in the winds
  covers over the sighing.
The cross shakes.
The earth shakes.
The graves shake.
The shaking blinds us
  until the Savior's blood
  washes away our sins,
  our fears and our blindness.
Now we can see the nails,
  the spears, the dice.

Once opened,
  our eyes shiver
  at the sight
  of a wooden cross
  where hangs our salvation.
Once opened,
  we wash our feet in shame.
Once opened,
  we grovel in our iniquity.

Easter Morning, April 20, 2003

Rising from the dead is no small matter.
It doesn't happen too often,
  and when it did happen once
  not surprisingly the event was recorded as holy text.
The event was no small matter
  to a small number of people
  who expected it and weren't surprised
  when the risen savior appeared to reliable witnesses,
  which is no small matter.
But in the scheme of things,
  it was the dying that was important
  because we all can die only once,
  and none of us is going to rise and speak to any witnesses.
It was the dying that cleansed the world
  and made up for all our sins.
It was the last words, the agony and the dying
  that we treasure because we must
  in our hope of resurrection into an afterlife.
Death comes to us all.
Resurrection happens only to a son of God,
  which is no small matter.

I Am the Resurrection and the Life

It was exhilarating
  to find myself rising
  at the thought of Resurrection.
Who would have believed
  that a dry run of eternal salvation
  was possible?
But there I was,
  rising over a graveyard,
  floating over a freeway
  and entering a fist-sized cloud
  with my name on it.
As I rose in the cloud,
  I felt as though
  I was enlarging,
  puffing out into a balloon of moisture
  until I could not contain myself.
It was exhilarating
  to let my rain fall on the dry world.
Then I knew that when the time would come
  for my final ascending,
I would be able to look out
  from my heavenly home
And celebrate the lilies
  that would grow tall
In my Second Coming.

Georg Trakl's "Psalm"

Transl. Dallas Wiebe

There is a light which the wind has snuffed out.
There is a wooden jug, which a drunk abandoned
    in the afternoon.
There is a vineyard, charred and black with holes
    full of spiders.
There is a room, which they have whitewashed
    with milk.
The idiot is dead. There is an island in the Pacific,
To receive the Sun God. Drums are beaten.
The men break into a war dance.
The women rock their haunches in creepers and
    fire flowers
When the sea sings. Oh our lost paradise.

                    *

The nymphs have departed from the golden woods.
The stranger is buried. Then a shivering rain begins.
The son of Pan appears in the form of a ditch digger
Who slumbers exhaustedly at noon on the glowing
    asphalt.
There are little girls in a courtyard in dresses full
    of heart-rending poverty.
There are rooms, filled with sonatas and chords.
There are shadows, which embrace each other in
    front of a blind mirror.
Convalescents warm themselves at the windows of
    the hospital.
A white steamer hauls bloody plagues up the canal.

*

The strange sister appears again in someone's angry
    dreams.
She plays with his stars while resting in the hazel
    bush.
The student, perhaps a Doppelgänger, watches her
    intently from his window.
Behind him stands his dead brother, or he goes down
    the old winding stair.
In the shade of the brown chestnut the figure of the
    young novice fades away.
The garden is of the evening. In the cloister bats
    flutter around.
The children of the concierge stop their games to
    search for the gold of heaven.

A quartet ends. The blind girl runs shivering
    through the narrow street,
And later her shadow gropes along cold walls,
    surrounded by fairy tales and holy legends.

*

There is an empty barge that drifts down the black
    canal at night.
In the gloom of the old asylum human wrecks decay.
Dead orphans lie along the garden wall.
From gray rooms step angels with filth-spattered
    wings.
Worms drop from their yellowed eyelids.
The church square is dark and silent, as in the days
    of our youth.
Former lives glide by on silver soles
And the shadows of the damned descend into the
    sighing waters.
In his grave the white magician toys with his snakes.
        *

On Golgotha, God's golden eyes open silently.

Trinity Heights Methodist Church Cross

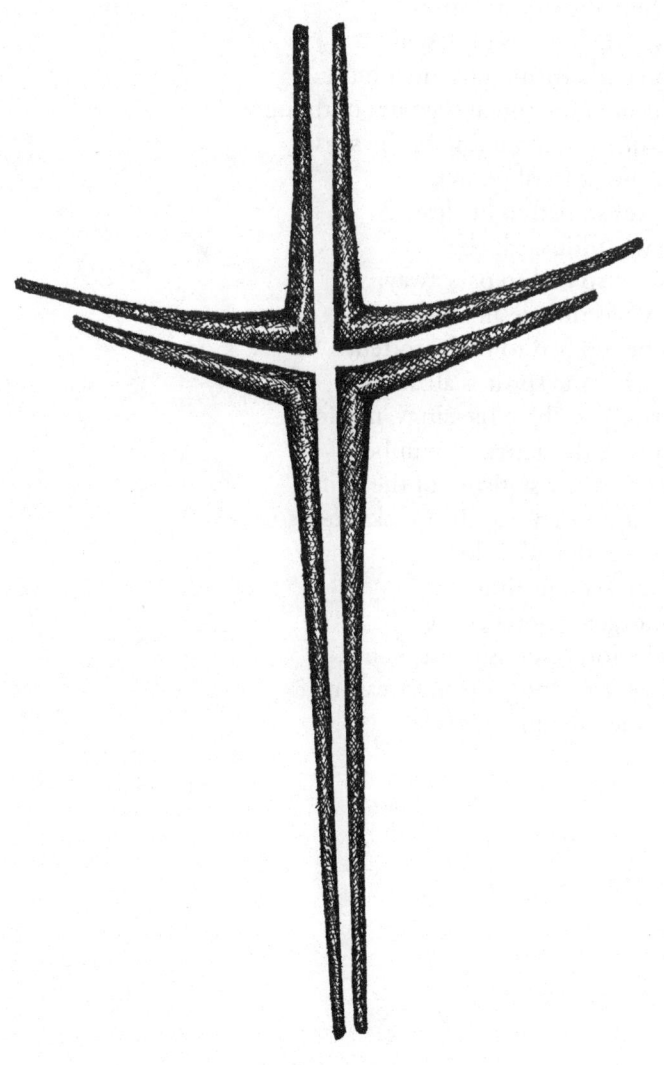

The New Order

Oh sweet peace of the dream world
  where the mind flutters
  over the images of despair.
Oh gentle turning of the mind
  through the fun and games of thought.
Oh quiet maundering of the senses
  in the sleep of reason.
It's not so bad to be dead;
It's what life is all about.
It's not so bad to pass away;
It's what time is all about.
It's not so bad to be forgotten;
It's what the spirit is all about.
I leave you three blessings, nay four.
Smile at the actuarial numbers.
Laugh at the statistics of the living.
Shout nonsense at the quick fixes.
Cry out that all is lost
And it's about time.
To forget is not a crime.
To be forgotten is not a shame.
To exist no longer is not treason
  to the human endeavor.

I tell you friends on the short list,
   that once committed
   you're twice shy,
   that as you calculate
   you're over the hill,
   that as you hope
   you are the evidence of things unseen.
To be nothing is the help of the helpless.
It is the dream that abides.

Yea, Though I Walk

For Virginia M. Wiebe (1929-2002)

In the valley of the shadow
  the road to the pit
  is deep and invisible.
In the valley of the shadow
  there is no air and no wind,
  there are no clouds and no sky.
In the valley of the shadow
  you wander,
  hands before your breast,
  feet groping over rocks.
The emptiness in the valley
  is filled with you
  and your sober mind.
It is filled with your unspoken words
  and your unfeeling skin.
It is filled with unheard-of sounds
  and your senseless eyes.
It is filled
  with the residue of your thinking
  and your grim words.
The shadow in the valley
  is there without sun.
The shadow in the valley
  is there without reflection.

The shadow in the valley
  is there because of you.
It is the shadow of the cross
  that covers your stumbling
  and that sanctifies the darkness.
In the holy shade
  there are no questions
  because there are no answers.
There is only you, the shadow
  and the cross.

INRI

In his hands
the iron nails.
In his side
the iron spear.
On his head
a crown of thorns.
In his arid mouth the final words.
In his long-suffering the first offering.
In his slow death the first redemption.
In his sight
the standing mother.
In his nostrils
the whiff of Rome.
In his ears
the babbling mob.
In his mouth
the sour drink.
In his dying
the wind of eternity.
In his burial
the promise of life.
In his resurrection the sign we all awaited.
In his ascension the rising of our souls.

The Author

Dallas Wiebe was born January 9, 1930, in Newton, Kansas. He grew up in Newton, attending public schools and graduating from Newton High School in 1948. He attended Bethel College and in 1954 received his B.A. in English Literature. From 1954 to 1960 he studied literature at the University of Michigan, receiving his M.A. in 1955 and his Ph.D. in 1960.

Wiebe taught literature and writing at the University of Wisconsin (Madison) 1960-1963 then moved to the University of Cincinnati until retiring from teaching in 1995. He continues to live and work in Cincinnati, Ohio.

His publications include the Mennonite novel *Our Asian Journey* (mlr editions canada, 1997), a book of minimalist poems called *The Kansas Poems* (Cincinnati Poetry Review Press, 1987), and four books of short stories. He has also had many short stories and poems released in various journals.

Wiebe married Virginia Schroeder in 1951. They have a son, a daughter, and five grandsons.

The Artists

Paul A. Friesen was born in Newton, Kansas, in 1923. He lived with his missionary parents in India from 1923 to 1941 where he attended Woodstock School in Landour, Mussoorie, India. He studied at Hesston College 1942-44 and Goshen College 1944-1946, receiving an A.B. degree. His other studies include study at the Goshen College Seminary (Th.B., 1946-47), post graduate work at Wichita University (1956-1957), and Fort Hays State University (M.S.in Art Education, 1958-1960). He served pastorates at East Peoria, Illinois (1947-1951) and West

Sterling, Illinois (1951-1956). He taught at Hesston College from 1956 to 1978 and at Bethel College from 1960 to 1989. His artwork includes exhibits in numerous national and regional shows. He has also exhibited in numerous invitational exhibits. He has received and accomplished over thirty commissions for churches, corporations, educational institutions and private homes. He currently is retired and resides with his wife in Schowalter Villa in Hesston, Kansas, where he is artist-in-residence. His most recent commission was for a sculpture for the new Women's Center in the Newton Medical Center. The sculpture was dedicated and unveiled on October 1, 2004.

John Leon is a free lance sculptor who lives and works in Cincinnati, Ohio. He was born in Cincinnati in 1955 and attended Cincinnati public schools. After he graduated from Walnut Hills High School he studied art at the University of Cincinnati and the Cincinnati Art academy. He currently teaches sculpture at the Art Academy part-time.

Leon has been a professional sculptor since 1980. His works in bronze, stone, and wood are in over four hundred private, public and corporate collections in Canada, England, Costa Rica, Greece, Saudi Arabia, and the U.S. He has exhibited widely in museums and galleries internationally, including Brookgreen Gardens, the National Sculpture Society, and the Costa Rican-North American Cultural Center.

Leon has been commissioned by Procter and Gamble, The Cincinnati Zoo, the Fort Lupton, Colorado, Fire Department, John Logan College, Wright Patterson Air Force Base, and many others. His work is represented by Bryant Galleries in New Orleans, Heike Pickett Galery in Lexington, Kentucky, and Willford and Vogt Fine Art in Santa Fe. He has been featured in *American Artist Magazine* and *Sculptural Pursuit*.

Made in the USA
Monee, IL

Made in the USA
Monee, IL
07 July 2026

56552022R00056